WORKBOOK

FOR

THE UNIVERSAL CHRIST

How a Forgotten Reality Can Change
Everything We See, Hope For, and Believe

BY RICHARD ROHR

Growth Hack Books

TABLE OF CONTENTS

CHAPTER 1: CHRIST IS NOT JESUS'S LAST NAME

SUMMARY

There are many different views on Jesus. In scripture, Peter first addresses the crowds and proclaims that God made Jesus not only Lord but also Christ. But what does that mean exactly? In order to understand that, we need to understand God and what happened during creation. Of course, we may never know how or when it happened but religion seems to try to tackle why.

Almost all traditions seem to believe that everything we know came from that Primal Source which was once only Spirit. Somehow, this Spirit made itself into every rock, tree, plant and human on the planet. With this, most Christians think of the birth of Jesus when they hear the word "incarnation". With this book, I want to explore the idea that rather than God joining humanity at the birth of Jesus that instead it was at the very beginning in Genesis 1.

Christ was hinted at in John 1:3 and long before Jesus himself was created. John's gospel says that light is not what you see but how you see everything else. Scientists have actually learned that the darkness that humans see with their eyes is not total darkness like we believe. It's actually made up of tiny particles which are actually slivers of light, we just can't see them. The symbolism is extremely apparent as light and goodness are mentioned often.

Because of this, the world can be seen differently. That even in the darkest moments, there was light. That there was a purpose, even for the worst of things. God loves things by becoming them, and he is supposed to be in all things. The Bible tells us that it doesn't matter what we call God, it's how we connect with Spirit. If we don't see that God is in everything, we can struggle to connect and end up feeling lonely.

Religion and beliefs have muddied up the waters of something that is simple and clear. Christ is a word for all that is good and complete. Jesus is the human representation of that. He shows that humans are capable, even if we don't realize it yet.

KNOWLEDGE RETENTION TEST

1. There is only one view of Jesus.

   True [ ]
   False [ ]

2. Religion has explained how everything was made.

   True [ ]
   False [ ]

3. God is also known as Spirit.

   True [ ]
   False [ ]

4. Spirit is only in things that are breathing.

   True [ ]
   False [ ]

4. Darkness is actually made up of particles of light we can't see.

   True [ ]
   False [ ]

PREP WORK Q & A

1. What did Peter mean when he said God made Jesus not only Lord but Christ?

\
\
\
\
\
\
\
\

2. What is the primal source everything is believed to have come from?

\
\
\
\
\
\
\
\

3. How has religion made understanding Jesus and God difficult?

\
\
\
\
\
\
\
\

CHECKLIST

____Think about why we may never know how creation happened.

____Ponder why all religions seem to believe in one Primal Source.

____Consider that even in places dark to the human eye, there is light.

____Understand that Christ is a word for all that is good and complete.

RECAP OF CHAPTER 1

1. Jesus and Christ are two separate things.

2. God is in everything in our world.

3. Jesus is the one who showed us that humans can be wholly connected.

CHAPTER 2: ACCEPTING THAT YOU ARE FULLY ACCEPTED

SUMMARY

I don't feel that Jesus was speaking about himself as Christ. I think it stands to reason he was speaking about the Christ consciousness. God is in all of us, so we can never fully know ourselves without also getting to know God. Starting off work on believing that Jesus and God were one. Then, start to understand that you and God are also one. After that, let it sink in that everything and God are also one.

The main message here is that God is in all of us, that's the lesson of the incarnation of God into Jesus. God needed someone to help get his point across faster. That's where Jesus came in. There are moments in scripture that point out that God is in the ordinary and that we don't need a big moment to see it.

Jesus said that people were the light of the world, but I think it's less direct. It's more of how you see rather than what. Christ didn't just come when incarnated into Jesus. It's been happening with every person. Christ allows people to see the light in everything and everyone. Many other religions have actually been able to embody Christ much better than many Christians. God doesn't have a favorite among religions. God doesn't have a gender or a name. We may call God a "he" but that is just because our minds tend to want to put a label on things. God doesn't care what name you use. As long as it's in your heart.

KNOWLEDGE RETENTION TEST

1. Jesus was speaking of himself when talking about Christ.

   True [ ]
   False [ ]

2. God is in the ordinary things.

   True [ ]
   False [ ]

3. Christ didn't just incarnate with Jesus.

   True [ ]
   False [ ]

4. God is neither male nor female.

   True [ ]
   False [ ]

5. Christians are the only ones that embody Christ correctly.

   True [ ]
   False [ ]

PREP WORK Q & A

1. What does it mean to be like Christ?

_____

_____

_____

_____

_____

_____

_____

2. Who and what are one with God?

_____

_____

_____

_____

_____

_____

_____

3. What does it mean that God is in the ordinary?

_____

_____

_____

_____

_____

_____

CHECKLIST

____Think about if you agree that Jesus was not referring to himself when speaking of Christ.

____Consider how you and God are one.

____Think about how God is in the ordinary moments.

____Think about why God doesn't have a favorite religion.

RECAP OF CHAPTER 2

1. Jesus was not referring to himself when speaking of Christ.

2. You and God are one.

3. God doesn't care what name or gender you assign to "him".

4. God is in everyone and everything.

CHAPTER 3: REVEALED IN US - AS US

SUMMARY

In the book of Acts, we're told about Saul and his conversion. He started out persecuting anyone who dared follow Jesus. On his way to Damascus he was suddenly blinded by "light". That light asked why he was persecuting him. When Saul asked who it was, the voice said it was Jesus and once again asked why he was being persecuted. Jesus saw no difference between Saul persecuting people who followed him and himself. After that, Saul was completely changed and became almost obsessed with Christ and changes his name to Paul.

Like Paul, we can never know Jesus but we can come to know Christ through ourselves. Moving from a place of sadness and separateness to one of fullness. Instead of thinking in terms of "I" beginning to think in terms of "we".

In the Gospel of Mark, Jesus instructs them to tell the Good News to every creature, not just humans. Why else would he do that unless they were all important? You have never actually been separated from God, only in your mind. So, in the beginning, Paul understood that there was something of a Christ consciousness but over time, Christians seemed to have lost that. It may seem like a big idea to expect others to shift to the idea of a Cosmic Christ, but that doesn't mean it can't happen.

Of course, it seems in this day there are lines drawn everywhere. People are separated by ethnicity and more. But that's not what was originally taught. It was that we are all one and the same. Even when I look at my dog, I see the Divine staring back at me. Anything that pulls you out of yourself in a very positive way is working as if it were God looking back at you. That's why it's so important to fully accept those times.

KNOWLEDGE RETENTION TEST

1. Saul persecuted anyone that followed Jesus.

   True [ ]
   False [ ]

2. Jesus felt he was different from his followers.

   True [ ]
   False [ ]

3. The only way to know Christ is through Jesus.

   True [ ]
   False [ ]

4. In the Gospel of Mark, Jesus tells them to spread the Good News to all people.

   True [ ]
   False [ ]

5. Paul understood there was a Christ consciousness.

   True [ ]
   False [ ]

PREP WORK Q & A

1. How can people become separated from God?

_____

_____

_____

_____

_____

_____

_____

2. Why did Saul become obsessed with Christ?

_____

_____

_____

_____

_____

_____

_____

3. How can we come to know God?

_____

_____

_____

_____

_____

_____

_____

CHECKLIST

___ Think about why God said Saul was persecuting him rather than his followers.

___ Consider how the Christ consciousness is in everything.

___Begin to see it's not "I" but "we".

___Start to see how humanity has drawn lines to separate us all.

RECAP OF CHAPTER 3

1. God does not intend for you to separate yourself from others.

2. God is in all beings.

3. To separate yourself from others is to separate yourself from God.

CHAPTER 4: ORIGINAL GOODNESS

SUMMARY

You can see the Divine in nature if you take the time to look. It can be a tree or a vista. You can experience it anywhere and with anything. Nature works easily with God in a way that humans struggle with. God loves everything and it's noted in the Bible and yet we love to limit the concept of his love to just humans.

In order to start loving in a way that is close to how God does, start with the smallest thing and work up. It can be hard to love God if you have a strained relationship. Or even people for that matter. But you can love rocks, trees and the grass much more easily. It is said that if you hate anything, you don't love God. That you can't hate one thing and not the other.

Humans were meant to enjoy everything and live in love with it all. Look at animals. They love with their whole hearts, trust in God and their place in this world. They don't have quite the fear of death that humans do.

The idea of original sin has gotten things twisted. It suggests that at some point you are able to not be a part of God. That if someone does something wrong, they are not godly. It should be noted that sin isn't mentioned in the Bible. It suggests that because of Adam and Eve we are being punished for something we didn't even do. The story starts with goodness and that it was where everything could grow and be without shame.

Thanks to Augustine who brought about the concept of original sin, people started believing this darker version of Genesis 3 rather than the nicer Genesis 1. Then, Jesus was given attention for his death rather than his life. We were told that because he died, all of the sin was wiped away. But the concept of us all being flawed and sinners didn't make things better. It made things worse. We humans need to move past the fear-based beliefs we have been ingrained with and once again embrace the idea of an all loving God.

Studies show our minds latch onto the bad but let the good slip away. Because of this, we have to work at being positive. It isn't going to just happen overnight. We have to make a constant choice to choose positive thinking. From the start, faith, love and hope are within us. We have to practice this so that we are open to the goodness of God. We must learn to accept others in all their differences because even if they are the opposite of us, they still carry God within them.

KNOWLEDGE RETENTION TEST

1. You can experience God anywhere.

   True [ ]

   False [ ]

2. Love is only meant for humans.

   True [ ]

   False [ ]

3. The idea of original sin suggest we are separated from God.

   True [ ]

   False [ ]

4. Peter brought about the idea of original sin.

   True [ ]

   False [ ]

5. Our minds automatically latch onto the bad.

   True [ ]

   False [ ]

PREP WORK Q & A

1. How can one begin to love the way God does?

_____

_____

_____

_____

_____

_____

_____

2. Why should we try to be more like animals?

_____

_____

_____

_____

_____

_____

_____

3. How did the concept of original sin get twisted?

_____

_____

_____

_____

_____

_____

_____

CHECKLIST

___Consider all the places you can see the Divine at work.

___Think about how animals are more like God than humans.

___Begin to work on loving all things.

___Work on paying more attention to the good and less attention to the bad.

RECAP OF CHAPTER 4

1. The Divine is in everything.

2. No one is truly without God's love.

3. Only when you love and accept others for who they are, can you be like God.

4. We should do our very best to focus on the positive in others and the world.

CHAPTER 5: LOVE IS THE MEANING

SUMMARY

Pierre Teilhard de Chardin was not only a priest but a scientist. He felt as though love actually made up the universe. He felt it was what drew all things together and helped unify some things on a much deeper level. Each different type of energy coming toward one another was a form of love.

The fact of the matter is, we all know and accept that love is a universal thing. It's not done differently in other religions or races. We all know what it feels like to have it in our lives.

Religion, when done right, can help bring divine love into their lives. It helps people wake up to what is surrounding us at all times. Yet our way of life tends to be one that tries to separate us from that feeling. We're taught we must win and be individual. But the truth is, we all need something or someone to love. It can drive us to do things and give us focus. No matter where we are, we need that human connection.

God uses all things to teach us love. It could start as something simple like the love of a clean house. God doesn't need all of the credit and love. When Jesus healed people, he did not pick and choose who would be healed based on their worthiness. And he never took credit for the healing either. He didn't brag or boast. Instead, he insisted that the person's faith did the work.

If you think about when you love someone, you don't freely give it. Most of the time, it's almost as if they take it from you. Their goodness or inner beauty will start a loving flow from you to them. It's like a loving electrical charge that is pulled from you. When sin is present, it cuts off that charge. But that absence can be what shows you just how important that love really is.

When it feels as though God is pulling away, it's just a part of the dance. We as humans are in a dance with the divine and with each step, we can move with, towards or away from the divine and the opposite is also true. We can only know how important something is, when it pulls away. In those moments, we must trust that God isn't actually gone or retreating. It's simply a step in the dance.

KNOWLEDGE RETENTION TEST

1. Pierre Teilhard de Chardin believed love brought all things together.

   True [ ]

   False [ ]

2. Love is done differently depending on religion and race.

   True [ ]

   False [ ]

3. It's important to stay separated from others.

   True [ ]

   False [ ]

4. Jesus never took credit for healing others.

   True [ ]

   False [ ]

5. God doesn't pull away, it's part of the dance.

   True [ ]

   False [ ]

PREP WORK Q & A

1. How does love bring everything together?

_____

_____

_____

_____

_____

_____

_____

2. How does our way of life inhibit love?

_____

_____

_____

_____

_____

_____

_____

3. How is love taken from you? List several ways.

_____

_____

_____

_____

_____

_____

_____

CHECKLIST

____Consider how love brings things together.

____Think about how religion done right brings us divine love.

____Think about how God uses all things to teach us to love.

____Contemplate how Jesus didn't take credit for healing others.

RECAP OF CHAPTER 5

1. Love of some form is what draws all things together.

2. God wants us to experience love because it draws us to him.

3. When it feels as though God is moving away, it's important to remember it's just a part of the dance.

CHAPTER 6: A SACRED WHOLENESS

SUMMARY

There are many that, over the years, have seemed to feel Christ's presence. One woman, who was killed in Auschwitz wrote about him often and her ability to feel him. What seems to be most striking is the fact that he tends to work right alongside what most would consider very negative circumstances. God seems to take those moments to help us see that he is still there. That love and suffering often work together so that you can see just how powerful they can be.

Unfortunately, it seems as though most feel that God is someone who punishes and shames us. Therefore, as we supposedly live in his image, we continue with the shaming and punishing. Carl Jung felt we all had a God Archetype within us that was a bit of God that was within ourselves.

Many people just aren't willing to submit themselves to the voice of God. They aren't willing to keep an open mind to the fact that he may not be what people once believed. When they hear that voice of intuition deep within themselves, they often believe it's their own thoughts and are unwilling to consider that it may be God. Joan of Arc accepted the voices as God and when she was accused of being a victim of her own imagination, asked the judge "How else would God speak to me?"

Many over the years have discovered that by turning inward, they were able to connect with God on a deeper level. By going inward, they found a trust in God. That voice is humble and tender which is how you can identify it. If it's full of bravado, it is not. If it tells you that you need to control others, then it's not God's voice, it's your own.

Practice will help you eventually see the flow of the positive in your mind and the resistance which is negative.

KNOWLEDGE RETENTION TEST

1. Only special people feel Christ's presence.

   True [ ]

   False [ ]

2. God is someone who punishes and shames us.

   True [ ]

   False [ ]

3. Turning inward brings you closer to God.

   True [ ]

   False [ ]

4. God's voice inside you is loud and demanding.

   True [ ]

   False [ ]

5. Practice will help you determine what is God's voice and what is your own.

   True [ ]

   False [ ]

PREP WORK Q & A

1. How do love and suffering work together?

_____

_____

_____

_____

_____

_____

_____

2. Why are so many people unwilling to submit to the voice of God?

_____

_____

_____

_____

_____

_____

_____

3. In what way does turning inward help you hear God?

_____

_____

_____

_____

_____

_____

_____

CHECKLIST

____Think about how love and suffering can go hand in hand.

____Come up with others you think may have heard the voice of God.

____Think back on times when you may have heard the voice of God.

____Understand what God's voice would sound like within yourself.

RECAP OF CHAPTER 6

1. Christ is within all of us.
2. You can hear his voice if you turn inward.
3. The voice of God is humble.
4. If the voice you hear is full of bravado, it's not God.

FUN BREAK 1 OF 3

Congrats, you're working hard so you've earned a little fun break. You'll notice 3 such fun breaks within this workbook, each with a different difficulty level. All of the words below should be familiar as they are taken from this book. Give your brain a mini vacation then jump back into learning. (Answers on next page)

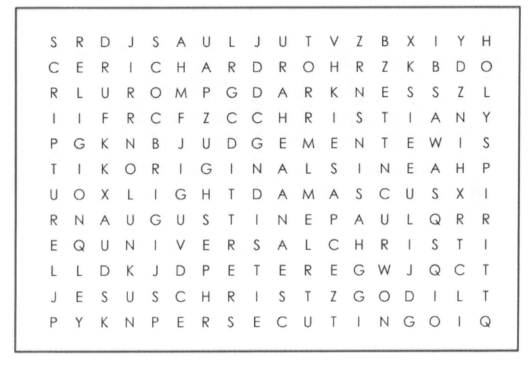

```
S  R  D  J  S  A  U  L  J  U  T  V  Z  B  X  I  Y  H
C  E  R  I  C  H  A  R  D  R  O  H  R  Z  K  B  D  O
R  L  U  R  O  M  P  G  D  A  R  K  N  E  S  S  Z  L
I  I  F  R  C  F  Z  C  C  H  R  I  S  T  I  A  N  Y
P  G  K  N  B  J  U  D  G  E  M  E  N  T  E  W  I  S
T  I  K  O  R  I  G  I  N  A  L  S  I  N  E  A  H  P
U  O  X  L  I  G  H  T  D  A  M  A  S  C  U  S  X  I
R  N  A  U  G  U  S  T  I  N  E  P  A  U  L  Q  R  R
E  Q  U  N  I  V  E  R  S  A  L  C  H  R  I  S  T  I
L  L  D  K  J  D  P  E  T  E  R  E  G  W  J  Q  C  T
J  E  S  U  S  C  H  R  I  S  T  Z  G  O  D  I  L  T
P  Y  K  N  P  E  R  S  E  C  U  T  I  N  G  O  I  Q
```

Find the following words in the puzzle.
Words are hidden → ↓ and ↘ .

AUGUSTINE	JUDGEMENT	SAUL
CHRISTIAN	LIGHT	SCRIPTURE
DAMASCUS	ORIGINALSIN	UNIVERSALCHRIST
DARKNESS	PAUL	
GOD	PERSECUTING	
HOLYSPIRIT	PETER	
JESUSCHRIST	RELIGION	
	RICHARDROHR	

FUN BREAK 1 OF 3 ANSWER SHEET

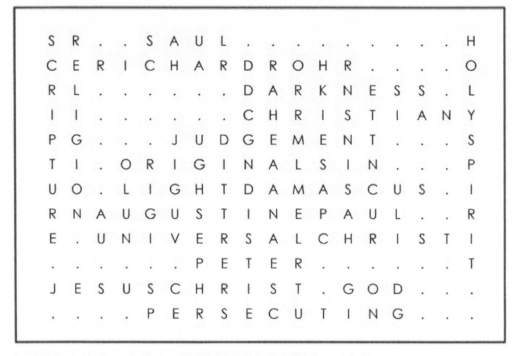

```
S  R  .  .  S  A  U  L  .  .  .  .  .  .  .  .  H
C  E  R  I  C  H  A  R  D  R  O  H  R  .  .  .  .  O
R  L  .  .  .  .  .  .  D  A  R  K  N  E  S  S  .  L
I  I  .  .  .  .  .  .  C  H  R  I  S  T  I  A  N  Y
P  G  .  .  .  J  U  D  G  E  M  E  N  T  .  .  .  S
T  I  .  O  R  I  G  I  N  A  L  S  I  N  .  .  .  P
U  O  .  L  I  G  H  T  D  A  M  A  S  C  U  S  .  I
R  N  A  U  G  U  S  T  I  N  E  P  A  U  L  .  .  R
E  .  U  N  I  V  E  R  S  A  L  C  H  R  I  S  T  I
.  .  .  .  .  .  P  E  T  E  R  .  .  .  .  .  .  T
J  E  S  U  S  C  H  R  I  S  T  .  G  O  D  .  .  .
.  .  .  .  P  E  R  S  E  C  U  T  I  N  G  .  .  .
```

Word directions and start points are formatted: (Direction, X, Y)

(SE,)
AUGUSTINE (E,3,8)
CHRISTIAN (E,9,4)
DAMASCUS (E,9,7)
DARKNESS (E,9,3)
GOD (E,13,11)
HOLYSPIRIT (S,18,1)
JESUSCHRIST (E,1,11)

JUDGEMENT (E,6,5)
LIGHT (E,4,7)
ORIGINALSIN (E,4,6)
PAUL (E,12,8)
PERSECUTING (E,5,12)
PETER (E,7,10)
RELIGION (S,2,1)
RICHARDROHR (E,3,2)

SAUL (E,5,1)
SCRIPTURE (S,1,1)
UNIVERSALCHRIST (E,3,9)

CHAPTER 7: GOING SOMEWHERE GOOD

SUMMARY

You may be wondering what the point of it all is and where it's going. After all, if Christ being within you is the beginning, then what is the end? You might think it's Armageddon and the earth being destroyed in fire. But fire isn't just destructive. It's also a tool for renewal.

You can look at it as a sort of evolution, although many Christians wouldn't like that word. It's all leading us somewhere with God as the focus point. Change takes time and it's important to remember that. People can't just change in an instant. Plants and animals have evolved in a way that seems to be planned out. Richard Dawkins, a biologist and atheist even admitted that evolution is too perfect to be some sort of random chance.

God seems to be the one in control, guiding everything to where it needs to go. And if you think about it, as Albert Einstein said, not just one thing is a miracle, all of it is. Even resurrection is something to consider, but perhaps not in the way traditionally thought. After all, every time you inhale, it's as if you are pulling spirit into matter and repeating the creation of Adam. When you exhale, you are allowing it to return to the universe. Much like a "little death" we have to release to continue on.

KNOWLEDGE RETENTION TEST

1. The end is Armageddon.

   True [ ]
   False [ ]

2. There is no such thing as evolution with God.

   True [ ]
   False [ ]

3. Change takes time.

   True [ ]
   False [ ]

4. Albert Einstein said that everything is a miracle.

   True [ ]
   False [ ]

5. Every exhale is like a "little death" releasing the old.

   True [ ]
   False [ ]

PREP WORK Q & A

1. How can evolution have happened because of God?

_____

_____

_____

_____

_____

_____

_____

2. Why do you think Richard Dawkins thinks evolution is too perfect to have happened by chance?

_____

_____

_____

_____

_____

_____

_____

3. Why is resurrection something we should consider?

_____

_____

_____

_____

_____

_____

_____

CHECKLIST

___Think about how God being within you is a part of the beginning.

___Consider if the end isn't what we initially thought.

___Think about how God could be using evolution.

___Ponder how every inhalation is like a resurrection.

RECAP OF CHAPTER 7

1. Many believe the world will end in fire.

2. Perhaps the fire mentioned in the Bible was a metaphor.

3. Fire represents change.

CHAPTER 8: DOING AND SAYING

SUMMARY

In the Apostles' Creed, there is a huge jump from Jesus being born to being crucified and the only thing to represent his entire life is a single comma. This seems to downplay everything Jesus did in life. Of course, the creed also leaves out any mention of love or forgiveness. Instead it leaves us with nothing that seems actionable. Instead it seems to put a greater distance between God and humanity. The problem is that the message was clouded by certain people and what they desired the message to be.

It may not seem like it from some of the official creeds, but Jesus was more focused on what we did rather than what was said. In Matthew 21:28 - 31 is the story of two sons. One says he won't work in the vineyard but ends up doing so anyway. The other says he will but then never does. Jesus goes on to say that he preferred the act of doing. So even though the one brother said he wouldn't, he actually did. That was what counted.

I believe that in our modern times we need the Jesus that was real. The man who showed us what it was truly like to be human. And with him, we need a Christ that is big enough to hold everything together for us.

KNOWLEDGE RETENTION TEST

1. Most focus on Jesus's birth and death.

    True [ ]

    False [ ]

2. The Apostles' Creed gives actionable advice.

    True [ ]

    False [ ]

3. Jesus is more focused on what we say rather than what we do.

    True [ ]

    False [ ]

4. God's message has been clouded through the years.

    True [ ]

    False [ ]

5. Christ isn't big enough to hold everything together.

    True [ ]

    False [ ]

PREP WORK Q & A

1. What is flawed in The Apostles' Creed?

_____

_____

_____

_____

_____

_____

_____

2. Why did Jesus prefer someone saying they won't and then doing to someone who says they will but doesn't?

_____

_____

_____

_____

_____

_____

_____

3. Why do we need to focus on Jesus's life?

_____

_____

_____

_____

_____

_____

_____

CHECKLIST

___Take time to consider what the point of The Apostles' Creed may have been.

___Think about who may have clouded the message.

___Consider reading the story in Matthew 21:28 - 31.

___Think about how Jesus's life could help people be better to one another.

RECAP OF CHAPTER 8

1. Not enough focus has been put on Jesus' life.

2. Jesus himself said he preferred people who took action to those that said they would.

3. Some religious teaches are clouded by man's desire to control one another.

CHAPTER 9 THINGS AT THEIR DEPTH

SUMMARY

Why is it that Catholics when receiving communion often still turn toward the altar and bow? Do they not realize that it's meant to show that it's being transferred to them? They aren't the only ones. it seems that humanity is so focused on going up that they never paid attention to all the signs that say God came down to us. That was why he came to Jesus, so that he could be on earth with us. Jesus was how God tried out being a human.

Jesus dealt with all the things we do on a day to day basis. He had the typical life filled with love and troubles just like we all do. God is in everything, even the bad times. We can all become wounded and yet resurrected at the same time. Only with great sadness and also great love can we find our way back to God. We can't try to avoid this life and everything in it so that we can hurry up and meet God. That's not the way it works. This isn't about materialism. This is about experiencing all that life has to offer. After all, God loves by becoming things.

We are living in a world that has so many different ways to help us guide ourselves inward. There are plenty of ways that people can experience this and often it's in ways that might surprise. There are so many tools for us to travel inward, it would be a shame to not use them.

While you may feel like this is too much focus on what you experience, remember that Jesus and Paul defied others based on what they felt. They went against what was socially acceptable at the time in order to express what they felt God wanted. You may wonder how these two were actually able to get away with it. The thing to remember is that for the most part, they didn't. It wasn't until after they were gone that scholars and saints realized just where the information came from.

KNOWLEDGE RETENTION TEST

1. People forget that God came down to us.

   True [ ]

   False [ ]

2. Jesus was how God tried being a human.

   True [ ]

   False [ ]

3. Jesus did not have a normal life.

   True [ ]

   False [ ]

4. God is not there in the bad times.

   True [ ]

   False [ ]

5. Jesus and Paul did what others wanted.

   True [ ]

   False [ ]

PREP WORK Q & A

1. How can one become wounded and resurrected at the same time?

_____

_____

_____

_____

_____

_____

_____

2. Why can't we avoid sadness and still get to know God?

_____

_____

_____

_____

_____

_____

_____

3. What are some things that help people focus inward?

_____

_____

_____

_____

_____

_____

_____

CHECKLIST

___Understand that God isn't somewhere else.

___Consider how God is there even in the sad times.

___Think of activities that can help you turn inward.

___Remember that Jesus was considered different in his time also.

RECAP OF CHAPTER 9

1. The best way to experience Christ is through going within.

2. You don't need validation from others with what you experience.

3. You can connect with God within you using anything that helps you reflect on yourself.

CHAPTER 10: THE FEMININE INCARNATION

SUMMARY

This chapter may be a little tough for me as a man to truly write about, but I shall do my best. Feminine wisdom is so completely different from male wisdom that it seems that it would be detrimental to not speak of it. Jesus may have been male, but God doesn't have a gender. So, there are ways that the feminine side has been represented.

I believe Mary was chosen as this divine feminine because she symbolizes the first incarnation. She obviously wasn't the first, but she blends well with the entire concept. She was the one that birthed Jesus and brought him to the world. She represents all of humanity. She was your average person before she became the mother of Jesus.

I also believe it's because she is a mother figure. We expect our mothers to be patient, kind and forgiving. Everything we want from a God. Mary was changed from being a poor maiden in Nazareth to a woman who was clothed in beautiful and flowing colors. It seems simpler to identify with Mary rather than Jesus because she was just a normal person. She didn't do anything but trust. She is there in the story when she simply needs to trust. She shows us that God can't be forced on us and never comes unless invited.

We have needed the divine feminine for a while now. Everything has become too competitive and unbalanced. The feminine has had to work behind the scenes with grace and subtlety. It's much more powerful than it is given credit for.

KNOWLEDGE RETENTION TEST

1. Feminine wisdom is the same as masculine wisdom.

   True [ ]
   False [ ]

2. Mary symbolizes the feminine wisdom.

   True [ ]
   False [ ]

3. Mary wasn't considered special in her life.

   True [ ]
   False [ ]

4. It's harder to identify with Mary.

   True [ ]
   False [ ]

5. All Mary had to do was trust.

   True [ ]
   False [ ]

PREP WORK Q & A

1. Why is Mary associated with Feminine wisdom?

_____

_____

_____

_____

_____

_____

_____

2. How is feminine wisdom different than masculine?

_____

_____

_____

_____

_____

_____

_____

3. What makes feminine wisdom so powerful?

_____

_____

_____

_____

_____

_____

_____

CHECKLIST

___Think about the importance of feminine wisdom.

___Consider how Mary embodied this.

___Think about how you can implement feminine wisdom in your life.

___Consider why masculine can find feminine so fear inducing.

RECAP OF CHAPTER 10

1. The divine feminine is represented in Mary.

2. She is easier to identify with since she was just a normal person.

3. She didn't have to do anything, simply trust the word of God.

CHAPTER 11: THIS IS MY BODY

SUMMARY

When Jesus proclaimed "this is my body" it shocked many of his followers. Many seem to think of giving their body as an intimate and often sexual thing. Was that Jesus' point? He even insisted that "my flesh is real food, my blood is real drink" in John 6:55. Of course, he didn't mean this literally. But I think instead it meant more that God would offer himself as food for us.

This seems more to do with the fact that he wanted us to know him more than in just the mind. After all, love affairs are never just in the mental space, but physical as well. He was saying he was in all of it. The bread and the wine. This way, you are more able to become Christ-like because you are what you eat.

Moreover, the thought of drinking the wine as his blood is a way to become one with all whose blood has been spilled. It's shocking because that is what seems to be the only thing that truly sticks with us. The things that shock our systems and pull us out of our haze we walk around in. In this way, the bread and wine represent all of the elements of the universe. With the universe being the body of God, of course.

KNOWLEDGE RETENTION TEST

1. Jesus meant something sexual when he offered his body.

   True [ ]

   False [ ]

2. God offered his body as food so that others would take him in.

   True [ ]

   False [ ]

3. Jesus's words were meant to shock his followers.

   True [ ]

   False [ ]

4. Shocking words help pull us from ourselves and encourages us to remember.

   True [ ]

   False [ ]

5. The bread and wine represent all of the universe.

   True [ ]

   False [ ]

PREP WORK Q & A

1. Why did Jesus say that his body was food for them to eat?

_____

_____

_____

_____

_____

_____

_____

2. Why would Jesus want them to think of the wine as blood of those who have died?

_____

_____

_____

_____

_____

_____

_____

CHECKLIST

___Think about why Jesus would want to shock his followers.

___Consider why he would say "my flesh is real food; my blood is real drink".

___Think about how his followers may have taken his proclamation.

___Ponder if the point was that they were what they were eating.

RECAP OF CHAPTER 11

1. God wanted us to feel unified with him.

2. Jesus was doing his best to let people know that by eating, they were taking the universe into themselves.

3. Since God is the universe, you are taking him into yourself when you eat.

Wow your making great progress, keep it up. This crossword puzzle is a little harder than your last puzzle. Do your best to solve it without using the answer sheet on the next page. Once you're done let's get back to learning.

Across: →

3. The act of pardoning an offender
5. to engage in contemplation or reflection
8. A religion based on the worship of Jesus
10. A particular system of faith or worship
12. A person with a high degree of holiness
13. The author of this book
14. Being nailed to a cross until dead
15. The last book of the bible
16. The evaluation of evidence in a matter

Down: ↓

1. The third person in the holy trinity
2. Christian worship involving bread and wine
4. consequences of Adam and Eves rebellion
6. The boyhood home of Jesus
7. A specialist in a particular field
9. Rising from the dead
11. The first book of the bible

FUN BREAK 2 OF 3 ANSWER SHEET

Across: →

3. The act of pardoning an offender
5. to engage in contemplation or reflection
8. A religion based on the worship of Jesus
10. A particular system of faith or worship
12. A person with a high degree of holiness
13. The author of this book
14. Being nailed to a cross until dead
15. The last book of the bible
16. The evaluation of evidence in a matter

Down: ↓

1. The third person in the holy trinity
2. Christian worship involving bread and wine
4. consequences of Adam and Eves rebellion
6. The boyhood home of Jesus
7. A specialist in a particular field
9. Rising from the dead
11. The first book of the bible

CHAPTER 12: WHY DID JESUS DIE?

SUMMARY

If you look around the world, you can see cultures that have been scarred by absent, violent or unavailable fathers. Add to that the fact that God is portrayed as a father figure who is a tyrant and you can see why things are the way they are. The dominant explanation for why Jesus had to die is that God was cruel and wanted someone to pay for the sins of mankind. This made it appear that sometimes violence is necessary. The idea that Jesus chose to die for our sins is central to many religions.

Yet Jesus never punished anyone. He might have challenged them, but that was for their enlightenment. He wanted them to heal or have new insight. Of course, early Christians wanted a reason as to why he had to die. And at first it was a sacrifice that wasn't made to God, but to the devil. This may have made the devil seem much more powerful, but it also gave a scapegoat for the death of Jesus. But through it all, God still appeared to be someone who expected you to behave a certain way or be punished.

Yet a Franciscan school turned this belief around. Instead of believing that blood had to be spilled to reach God, they proposed that God spilled blood in order to reach us. It was shown to be something of an outpouring of love for us and make us return to God.

The belief in a punishing God seems to have had the opposite effect for some. We believe God wants to love us and for us to love him, so it makes it hard to believe he would do something so horrible. In the Gospels he even said he didn't want sacrifice but instead, mercy.

The problem instead lies in humanity. Here we have a mix of heaven and divine. Our world is filled with contradictions. Jesus understood that there had to be contradictions and that they must be fully embraced for what they are. That is what led to his resurrection. The pain and suffering can radically change perspective. It's far too easy to push the sin off onto something else instead and allow it to be the one that suffers.

Instead, Jesus was condemned as an innocent man by the highest authorities. This is something that still seems to be missed. The powers that be want us to focus on our personal sins and not on theirs. So, to follow Jesus, we should see him crucified and feel sympathy for all suffering. Allowing it to show us how we have all been affected by hate and violence.

KNOWLEDGE RETENTION TEST

1. The world has been scarred by absent fathers.

   True [ ]

   False [ ]

2. God is portrayed as a tyrant many times.

   True [ ]

   False [ ]

3. Jesus punished those who did wrong.

   True [ ]

   False [ ]

4. The idea that God is punishing is a human notion.

   True [ ]

   False [ ]

5. God doesn't want sacrifices, he wants mercy.

   True [ ]

   False [ ]

PREP WORK Q & A

1. How has humanity's father issues shaped God?

_____

_____

_____

_____

_____

_____

_____

2. Why did Jesus never punish anyone?

_____

_____

_____

_____

_____

_____

_____

3. Why was Jesus killed?

_____

_____

_____

_____

_____

_____

_____

CHECKLIST

___Consider how human beliefs have changed our view of God through the years.

___Think about who may have wanted to change the way we see God.

___Debate how Jesus's crucifixion has shaped our beliefs.

___Decide what you think the reason behind his death was.

RECAP OF CHAPTER 12

1. Viewpoints of why Jesus died on the cross have been twisted.

2. For too long the focus has been on individual sin when it should be on feeling sympathy.

3. Only in suffering can we truly feel closer to God.

CHAPTER 13: IT CAN'T BE CARRIED ALONE

SUMMARY

The world has become very twisted and sad. I had been struggling with all the negativity in the world and the sadness of losing my dog Venus. As everything seemed to pile on top of me, I fell into what could be called the Great Sadness. yet along the way I started to find my way out and realized that we are all in this suffering together. Everyone has their own hurts that they carry inside them, even if they don't realize it. This makes it easier to be kind to others.

The crucifixion therefore becomes a symbol of that one big suffering that God goes into with us. Not for us, but with us. it's even been said that there is no individual suffering, just our own part that we must carry with everyone else. In this way, we are all saved because we are all connected.

Our modern world has us feeling lonely. Scared and struggling in a world we think is out to get us. Because of this, people and the planet suffer for our ego. As long as each person feels their suffering is more important or somehow different than another's, we as a people will struggle.

KNOWLEDGE RETENTION TEST

1. The world has become a sad place.

    True [ ]

    False [ ]

2. Sadness shows us God.

    True [ ]

    False [ ]

3. Everyone suffers together.

    True [ ]

    False [ ]

4. Our world makes us feel lonely.

    True [ ]

    False [ ]

5. Nobodies suffering is greater than another's.

    True [ ]

    False [ ]

PREP WORK Q & A

1. How can suffering unite us?

_____

_____

_____

_____

_____

_____

2. How does believing our pain is worse than others keep us separated?

_____

_____

_____

_____

_____

_____

3. How can suffering help you see God?

_____

_____

_____

_____

_____

_____

CHECKLIST

____Think about why there is so much negativity in the world.

____Talk about any sadness you feel with someone you trust.

____See that all sadness is the same.

____Learn to reach out and embrace the sadness.

RECAP OF CHAPTER 13

1. Everyone suffers.
2. The idea that we are all individual is part of what has made us feel alone.
3. Seeing suffering as universal and something we all must carry our part of makes it easier to bear.

CHAPTER 14: THE RESURRECTION JOURNEY

SUMMARY

If we share our suffering, does that mean we share resurrection? It's argued that Jesus and his resurrection was not a one-time thing. Instead, Paul tried to express that universal message that Spirit is within us at all times.

Of course, science says that nothing stays the same. That our body is constantly replacing its atoms each year. If you think about it, resurrection is just another word for change. Most actually believe in some form or resurrection, even if they don't believe Jesus was brought back from the dead. After all, if matter is part of God then that means that matter is eternal. This would mean our bodies as well and not just Jesus.

But our human minds struggle with this. We seem to have difficulties understanding the first creation also. how can something just come from nothing? Our minds can't seem to wrap around that concept. Yet I think the struggle to prove he came back from the dead or not is missing the point. Besides, there is no way to ever scientifically prove it anyway.

With God being in the world around us, it is said that God can speak and listen to us. It is up to us if we want to believe what we are hearing. You don't even need to call it God, because God doesn't care what you call it.

For the majority of the first six centuries, that moment of Jesus's resurrection was considered uncarvable and unpaintable. There isn't much that speaks of what happened at resurrection. In the resurrection Jesus was revealed to be everyman and everywoman as in their fulfilled state. Jesus was supposed to show that divinity could reside in humanity. Of course, we always deny this and its one of our biggest issues. But if death is not possible for Christ, then it's also not possible for anything else that shares divine nature.

But many still see God as something of a Great punisher. There is mention of hell as a place that can be descended into. There are many variations of the fire and brimstone that supposedly comes with the wrath of God. Of course, our human minds don't understand love and forgiveness well. Even though it shows through the Bible how much that is wanted for us. At the end of everything, God makes sure to state how much he loves us.

If you are coming from a scarcity mindset, there will never be enough grace or God for everyone.

KNOWLEDGE RETENTION TEST

1. Jesus is not the only one to be resurrected.

    True [ ]

    False [ ]

2. Science says everything stays the same.

    True [ ]

    False [ ]

3. Matter is eternal.

    True [ ]

    False [ ]

4. Our human minds understand how something comes from nothing.

    True [ ]

    False [ ]

5. God only wants to be called one thing.

    True [ ]

    False [ ]

PREP WORK Q & A

1. How is resurrection a possibility?

_____

_____

_____

_____

_____

_____

_____

2. Why does the human mind struggle with resurrection?

_____

_____

_____

_____

_____

_____

_____

3. What happens if you have a scarcity mindset?

_____

_____

_____

_____

_____

_____

_____

CHECKLIST

___Consider that resurrection wasn't just for Jesus.

___Look up the scientific claim that matter never ends.

___Come to your own conclusions.

___Think about how you define God.

RECAP OF CHAPTER 14

1. Resurrection isn't what we traditionally think of it.
2. There is enough grace and God to go around.
3. Resurrection is promised to all, not just Jesus.

CHAPTER 15: TWO WITNESSES TO JESUS AND CHRIST

SUMMARY

There are two people in the Bible that can tell us more about Jesus and Christ. One being Mary Magdalene who knew him as a human and Paul who knew him as Christ.

Mary Magdalene became Jesus's follower after he cast demons from her. She was there when he was crucified and also the one that saw his body was gone from the tomb. When the apostles took off, she stayed to cry and weep for her friend and teacher. When she turns to see him, she doesn't recognize him at first. She was given the ability to be the first to see him as the more omnipresent Christ, making her the apostle of the apostles.

Paul, on the other hand, never knew Jesus as a man. He only knew him as the Risen Christ. His story is one of conversion and he went from his self-love to a group love and then on to universal love. he also never spoke of hell the way we think of it. Instead, it was more that we were punished by our sins instead of for them. he seemed to feel evil was more within things that were like corporations and institutions. Those things that are usually held unaccountable and sometimes even above the law. It's believed he felt the only way to fight this was with a corporate goodness which is why he is considered the founder of church.

Jesus never seemed overly worried about those bad behaviors we think of as sins. Instead he was more concerned about the people who didn't think they were sinners. And actually, Paul never speaks of individual guilt, we just take it that way.

KNOWLEDGE RETENTION TEST

1. Only one person knew Jesus well.

   True [ ]

   False [ ]

2. Mary Magdalene didn't know much about Jesus.

   True [ ]

   False [ ]

3. Paul knew Jesus well in life.

   True [ ]

   False [ ]

4. Jesus didn't like sinners.

   True [ ]

   False [ ]

5. Paul is considered the founder of the church.

   True [ ]

   False [ ]

PREP WORK Q & A

1. How can we learn more about Jesus from seeing how others knew him?

_____

_____

_____

_____

_____

_____

_____

2. In what way did Mary Magdalene know Jesus?

_____

_____

_____

_____

_____

_____

_____

3. How did Paul know Jesus?

_____

_____

_____

_____

_____

_____

_____

CHECKLIST

___Consider who Jesus may have been in life.

___Think about how different he may have become after his resurrection.

___Think about if you have ever had a resurrection moment.

___Consider why Jesus wasn't worried about personal sins.

RECAP OF CHAPTER 15

1. Two people can help us learn about Jesus, Mary Magdalene and Paul.

2. Mary Magdalene knew Jesus when he was just a man.

3. Paul knew Jesus as Christ. There was no focus on individual sins.

FUN BREAK 3 OF 3

You've made it to the final fun break. This one will really test your skill. The words below are all from this book and can be hidden across, down, diagonal and backwards. Enjoy the final fun break then let's get back to learning. (Answer sheet on next page)

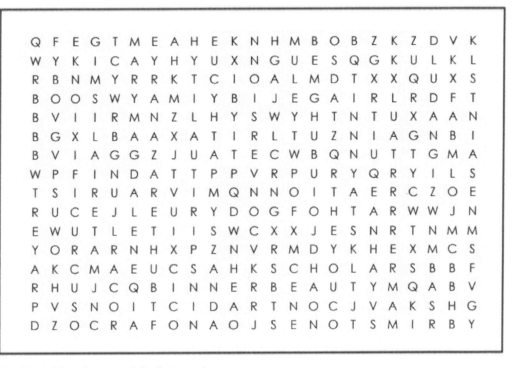

Find the following words in the puzzle.
Words are hidden ↑ ↓ → ← and ↘ .

BRIMSTONE
CARLJUNG
CONTRADICTIONS
CONVERSION
CREATION
CRUCIFIXION
HUMANITY

INNERBEAUTY
JOANOFARC
MARYMAGDALENE
MATERIALISM
MEDITATION
NAZARETH
PRAYER

SAINTS
SCHOLARS
SPIRITUALITY
STRUGGLE
SYMPATHY
WRATHOFGOD

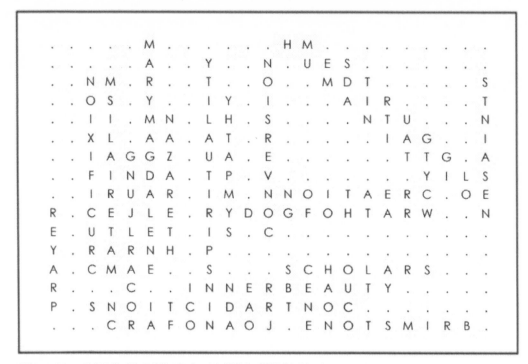

Word directions and start points are formatted: (Direction, X, Y)

BRIMSTONE (W,22,16)
CARLJUNG (N,5,14)
CONTRADICTIONS (W,16,15)
CONVERSION (N,12,11)
CREATION (W,20,9)
CRUCIFIXION (N,3,13)
HUMANITY (SE,13,1)

INNERBEAUTY (E,8,14)
JOANOFARC (W,12,16)
MARYMAGDALENE (S,6,1)
MATERIALISM (N,4,13)
MEDITATION (SE,14,1)
NAZARETH (S,7,5)
PRAYER (N,1,15)

SAINTS (N,23,8)
SCHOLARS (E,13,13)
SPIRITUALITY (N,9,13)
STRUGGLE (SE,16,2)
SYMPATHY (N,10,11)
WRATHOFGOD (W,20,10)

CHAPTER 16: TRANSFORMATION AND CONTEMPLATION

SUMMARY

For the longest time, humanity didn't see God in the broad view. It is a bit like trying to see the whole universe with just a telescope. We need to take the time to contemplate things in order to see them as they are. We tend to just see bits and pieces, only to try to fill in the rest.

It seems there is something new coming out of Christianity. It's a new humility from seeing our past mistakes. All of the indigenous people we hurt while trying to colonize as well as slavery. We now see the error of our ways. Nothing is ever black and white, although our human brains try to make it that way. We must accept what has happened and forgive ourselves while trying to move on from it.

God uses both love and suffering to teach us the lessons that matter. When we lose someone we love, we are completely changed by it, sometimes never returning to the person we were. The same can be with those in love. In these moments we are blown wide open and open to new ways.

Spirituality is all about loving and honoring the human journey. Living with all the tragedies and wonders it has to offer. Giving love when you can and connecting with the world and everything in it.

KNOWLEDGE RETENTION TEST

1. Humans have always seen the broad view of God.

   True [ ]

   False [ ]

2. God uses both love and suffering to teach us.

   True [ ]

   False [ ]

3. Spirituality is all about who can grow the fastest.

   True [ ]

   False [ ]

4. God has nothing to do with suffering.

   True [ ]

   False [ ]

5. Christians never made mistakes.

   True [ ]

   False [ ]

PREP WORK Q & A

1. Why does it seem as if humans see God through a telescope?

_____

_____

_____

_____

_____

_____

_____

2. How does God use both love and suffering to teach?

_____

_____

_____

_____

_____

_____

_____

3. What is spirituality all about?

_____

_____

_____

_____

_____

_____

_____

CHECKLIST

___Research different views of God in different religions.

___Consider how Christianity got things wrong.

___Think of ways to broaden your spirituality.

___See how God has used love and suffering to teach you in your life.

RECAP OF CHAPTER 16

1. For many years, Christianity got it wrong.

2. In our modern world, we are starting to accept what we've done wrong before.

3. The most important part is giving of yourself.

CHAPTER 17: BEYOND MERE THEOLOGY: TWO PRACTICES

SUMMARY

You may be wondering the point in all of this? My hope is that you can start to experience this Christ consciousness much sooner than I had the ability. At some point, we have to find a way that is comfortable to us for letting go. This can be some sort of prayer, meditation, or shadow work to find it. That's probably why so many people avoid personal contemplation because it's not a comfortable process. It can often feel like you are shedding an old and familiar skin. It can be hard for us to let go.

I noticed once that many things Christians do, the Native Americans also do. They burn sage for blessings and we burn incense. We do a sign of the cross and they draw the sun to their faces. The actions may be different but the meaning is the same.

The key point is to find a way to that place of complete trust and release. Where you don't worry about who you are or what you should be doing. Just accept that God is and so are you. Trust in that and it all seems to come together.

RETENTION CHECK

1. There is only one way to let go.

   True [ ]

   False [ ]

2. it's important to find the Christ consciousness within you.

   True [ ]

   False [ ]

3. Meditation can help you find God.

   True [ ]

   False [ ]

4. Most religions at their core believe the same things.

   True [ ]

   False [ ]

5. The important part is to trust.

   True [ ]

   False [ ]

PREP WORK Q & A

1. Why do most religions have similar practices?

_____

_____

_____

_____

_____

_____

_____

2. What are some ways you can learn to let go?

_____

_____

_____

_____

_____

_____

_____

3. How can you find a way to trust and release?

_____

_____

_____

_____

_____

_____

_____

CHECKLIST

___Begin to consider how you will find the Christ consciousness and connect.

___Try meditation.

___Look into shadow work.

___Research other ways people get in touch with themselves.

RECAP OF CHAPTER 17

1. Personal contemplation can be uncomfortable.

2. All religions have their own ways of connecting with God.

3. You can connect in whatever way works for you.

CHEAT SHEET

Recap of chapter 1

1. Jesus and Christ are two separate things.
2. God is in everything in our world.
3. Jesus is the one who showed us that humans can be wholly connected.

Recap of chapter 2

1. Jesus was not referring to himself when speaking of Christ.
2. You and God are one.
3. God doesn't care what name or gender you assign to "him".
4. God is in everyone and everything.

Recap of chapter 3

1. God does not intend for you to separate yourself from others.
2. God is in all beings.
3. To separate yourself from others is to separate yourself from God.

Recap of chapter 4

1. The Divine is in everything.
2. No one is truly without God's love.
3. Only when you love and accept others for who they are, can you be like God.
4. We should do our very best to focus on the positive in others and the world.

Recap of chapter 5

1. Love of some form is what draws all things together.
2. God wants us to experience love because it draws us to him.
3. When it feels as though God is moving away, it's important to remember it's just a part of the dance.

Recap of chapter 6

1. Christ is within all of us.

2. You can hear his voice if you turn inward.

3. The voice of God is humble.

4. If the voice you hear is full of bravado, it's not God.

Recap of chapter 7

1. Many believe the world will end in fire.

2. Perhaps the fire mentioned in the Bible was a metaphor.

3. Fire represents change.

Recap of chapter 8

1. Not enough focus has been put on Jesus' life.

2. Jesus himself said he preferred people who took action to those that said they would.

3. Some religious teaches are clouded by man's desire to control one another.

Recap of chapter 9

1. The best way to experience Christ is through going within.

2. You don't need validation from others with what you experience.

3. You can connect with God within you using anything that helps you reflect on yourself.

Recap of chapter 10

1. The divine feminine is represented in Mary.

2. She is easier to identify with since she was just a normal person.

3. She didn't have to do anything, simply trust the word of God.

Recap of chapter 11

1. God wanted us to feel unified with him.

2. Jesus was doing his best to let people know that by eating, they were taking the universe into themselves.

3. Since God is the universe, you are taking him into yourself when you eat.

Recap of chapter 12

1. Viewpoints of why Jesus died on the cross have been twisted.

2. For too long the focus has been on individual sin when it should be on feeling sympathy.

3. Only in suffering can we truly feel closer to God.

Recap of chapter 13

1. Everyone suffers.

2. The idea that we are all individual is part of what has made us feel alone.

3. Seeing suffering as universal and something we all must carry our part of makes it easier to bear.

Recap of chapter 14

1. Resurrection isn't what we traditionally think of it.

2. There is enough grace and God to go around.

3. Resurrection is promised to all, not just Jesus.

Recap of chapter 15

1. Two people can help us learn about Jesus, Mary Magdalene and Paul.

2. Mary Magdalene knew Jesus when he was just a man.

3. Paul knew Jesus as Christ. There was no focus on individual sins.

Recap of chapter 16

1. For many years, Christianity got it wrong.

2. In our modern world, we are starting to accept what we've done wrong before.

3. The most important part is giving of yourself.

Recap of chapter 17

1. Personal contemplation can be uncomfortable.

2. All religions have their own ways of connecting with God.

3. You can connect in whatever way works for you.

ABOUT GROWTH HACK BOOKS

Here at Growth Hack Books our goal is to save you time by providing the best workbooks possible. We stand out from our competitors by not only including all of the pertinent facts from the subject book but also knowledge retention tests after each chapter, a Prep work Q & A section after each chapter that allows you to document the steps you will take to reach your goals, easy to follow summaries of each chapter including checklists and even puzzles and games to make learning more interesting.

As you can see, we go above and beyond to make your purchase a pleasant one. If you learned something beneficial from this book please leave a positive review so others can benefit as well. Lastly if you haven't yet make sure you purchase the subject book, The Universal Christ, by visiting https://amzn.to/2Hasa83

Made in the
USA
Lexington, KY